My First Book About Dinosaurs

I0440681

Amazing Animal Books
Children's Picture Books

By Molly Davidson

Mendon Cottage Books

JD-Biz Publishing

Download Free Books!
http://MendonCottageBooks.com

All Rights Reserved.
No part of this publication may be reproduced in any form or by any means, including scanning, photocopying, or otherwise without prior written permission from JD-Biz Corp and http://AmazingAnimalBooks.com. Copyright © 2015
All Images Licensed by Fotolia, Pixabay, and 123RF

Read More Amazing Animal Books

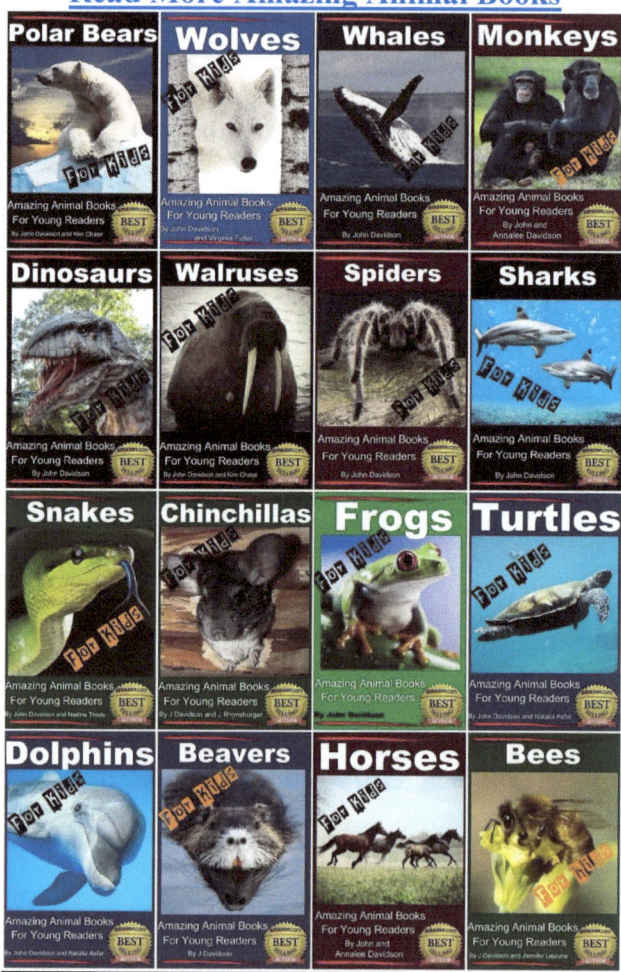

Download Free Books!
http://MendonCottageBooks.com

Table of Contents

Introduction to Dinosaurs

The word dinosaur comes from the ancient Greek word, denios, which means terrible lizard.

Dinosaurs ruled the Earth 65 to 225 million years ago.

Tyrannosaurus Rex

Facts about Dinosaurs

Have you ever heard of Dinosaurs? What are they?

Dinosaurs are reptiles that lived on earth over 230 million years ago.

Dinosaurs are extinct, they cannot be found alive today but their fossils are being found and studied.

Brachiosaurus

The heaviest dinosaur weighed about 80 tons (the weight of a whale), it was called brachiosaurus. Brachiosaurus had a height of 52 feet (that is a 5 story building) and a length of 85 feet (about two school buses).

Dinosaur laid eggs which can be found in many shapes.

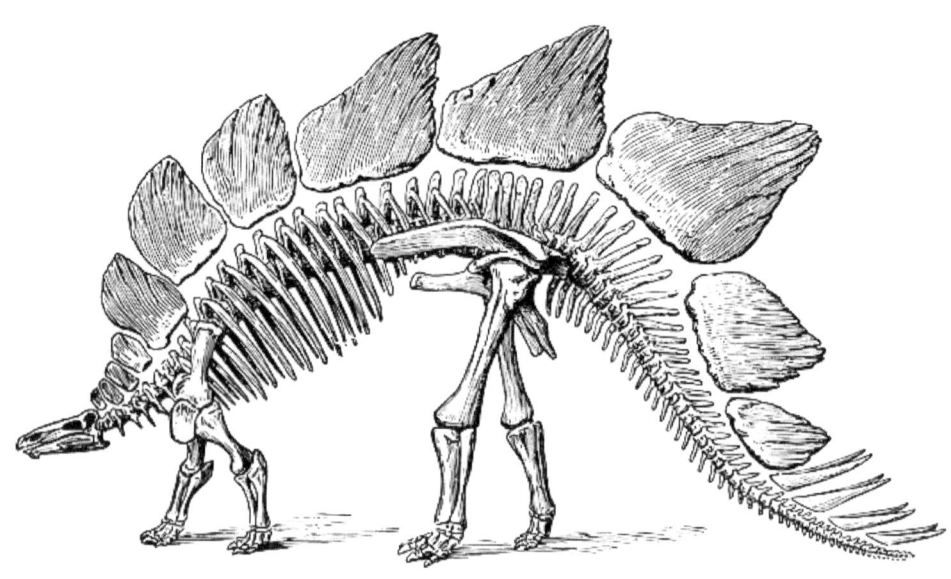

Troodon is the most intelligent dinosaur. Its brain

was equal to the brain of the today's animals; it could grab with its hands and saw in 3D.

Fight between Euoplocephalus tutus and Troodon formosus

Ostrich mimic ornithomiminds was the fastest dinosaur. It was able to run as fast as 37 miles per hour.

The oldest dinosaur fossils, which are 230 million years old, were found in Madagascar.

Micropachycephalosaurus is the longest name of a dinosaur which means tiny thick headed lizard.

There are over 700 species of dinosaurs that have been discovered so far.

Microraptor

Dinosaur Extinction

Dinosaurs became extinct, which means no more are living, 65 million years ago.

Since they became extinct so long ago, it is hard for scientists to tell us exactly why.

Once idea is there were too many volcanic eruptions in a short time, changing the weather, and the dinosaurs couldn't change, so they died.

Another idea is diseases could have spread rapidly among the dinosaurs killing all of them.

Kentrosaurus Dinosaurs

Third idea is an ice age, where the earth gets really cold, could have killed the dinosaurs, since they couldn't warm up.

Some other scientists think a very large asteroid hit the earth killing many plants, which took food away from the dinosaurs, so they died.

Tylosaurus

The best answer is probably that all of things happened, and the combination ended up killing all the dinosaurs.

Dinosaur Fossils

The most dinosaur fossils have been found in China, in a place called Shandong.

Another place in China known for fossils is Zhucheng city, which means the home of dinosaurs.

Dinosaur Fossil

In Britain, 108 species of dinosaurs have been discovered so far.

Dinosaur fossils are extremely breakable, so they are kept in museums and galleries for people to see, but not touch.

Many museums will make a model of the real fossils, and that is what they will display, so the real fossils are not damaged in any way.

Dinosaur Eggs

Dinosaur's eggs have been found all over the world.

Like the picture below the baby dinosaurs found in fossilized eggs can be studied to learn more about these wonderful animals.

Dinosaur Egg

What Dinosaurs Ate

Most dinosaurs ate plants; grass, trees, and roots. Plant eating animals are called herbivores.

Dinosaurs would sometimes swallow sand and rocks to help them digest their food. They would also drink lots of water and slept after eating.

Some dinosaurs ate meat; they would hunt down other animals. Meat eating animals are called carnivores.

Carnivore dinosaurs were bigger, faster, and stronger than the plant eating dinosaurs.

Suchomimus Dinosaurs

The last types of dinosaurs are ones that ate both plants and meat. These animals are called omnivores.

Omnivores are the fewest type of dinosaur. They would eat insects, birds, tree leaves, plants, and sometimes they would hunt bigger animals.

Dilophosaurus wetherilli

Feathered Dinosaurs

The discovery of a small skeleton by the Shandong Tianyu Museum suggests that some dinosaurs had feathers.

The scientist concluded that this dinosaur had feathers on its back, chest, and stomach.

Feathered dinosaurs are much bigger than our birds today, they ate meat and plants.

Archaeopteryx Dinosaur

Many of these feathers dinosaurs could not fly, the feathers were just to help keep them warm.

Plant Eating Dinosaurs

Herbivorous dinosaurs were well adapted with chewing teeth and long necks to enable them feed on plants.

1. Sauropodomorphs

They were able to feed on trees up to 4 feet tall.

They had teeth which were roughened and diamond shaped for easy tearing of vegetation.

2. Ornithischains

They had horny heads and backs, which were used for chopping plants down to eat.

3. Larger ornithopods

They had a beak which was sharp, interlocking teeth, and wide mouth for picking plant foods.

4. Larger ceratopsians

They had extremely narrow beak which were used to feed on vegetation by cutting the vegetation.

They had more than one hundred teeth behind the beak; the teeth were interlocking for easy chewing of plants.

The Weirdest Dinosaurs

Let's look at some dinosaurs that have traits that are very different from other dinosaurs.

#1. Oviraptor

They looked very similar to an ostrich. Other winged dinosaurs had more bat like wings, this one looked like a bird, and they even laid their eggs in a nest.

#2. Ouranosaurs

They had spines coming out of their backbone which may have meant they had weak skin, or it was fatty, like a camels hump.

#3. Carnotaurus

They are related to a T-Rex, they have tiny arms compared to their large bodies. They also have horns on their head, which they would use to head butt their prey.

#4. Suchomimus

Crocodiles are related to these dinosaurs. They were weird because they ate fish and meat, but their digestive system was like a plant eating dinosaur.

#5. Mamenchisaurus

A long neck dinosaur, but what is interesting is the length of their necks were 35 - 40 feet long!

They could not stretch their necks all the way out; it was too far to pump blood from the heart.

The Deadliest Dinosaurs

#1. Tyrannosaurus Rex

It was big in size; it had many strong and sharp teeth on its head. It could run really quick t catch its prey.

2. Utahraptor dinosaur

It had single curved claws which looked like knives.

#3. Jeholopterus

This dinosaur had sharp fangs. It is believed that the Jeholopterus ate by sucking blood from other dinosaurs.

4. Kronosaurus

This is believed to have been bigger than a great

white shark. It used to eat almost any creature that lived in the sea. It also attacked other land creatures that moved close to the waters where it used to stay.

#5. Troodon

Troodon were deadly but small, it weighs about the same as a human.

It didn't have sharp teeth like other deadly dinosaurs.

It was so intelligent that it used to hunt while in packs at night. A pack of 5 Troodon's could kill a T-Rex!

Troodons attacking a Euoplocephalus

#6. Sarcosuchus

They were twice as long as crocodiles today, and weighed 10 times more. It had a long neck and would jump out of the water to catch prey.

#7. Giganotosaurus

It weighed about 8.8 tons, and it was larger than any other meat eating dinosaur.

Flying Dinosaurs

Dimorphodon

Most reptiles now cannot fly, but back when the dinosaurs roamed, many were fliers.

#1. Dimorphodon

It has two kinds of teeth, is about 3 feet long, and has a wing span of 4 feet.

It could not walk, so if it was not flying, it would perch in a tree.

Rhamphorhynchus

#2. Rhamphorhynchus

They had short legs, a long tail, and its wing span was about 3 feet.

It had a skinny jaw with very sharp teeth and it had a beak so it could catch fish as it flew over water.

Quetzalcoatlus

#3. Quetzalcoatlus

It lived in North America and was one of the largest flying dinosaurs.

Its wing span was 36 feet in length, it had large eyes, a crested head, a very thin beak, and it weighed about 300 pounds.

The bones of this flying dinosaur were hallow and it also had very strong wings, so it could fly for long distances.

#4. Pterodactylus

They lived by water and ate fish and other kinds of small animals.

Its wing span was 20 to 30 inches and this reptile had wings that were covered with a strong membranes.

Kinds of Dinosaurs

Dinosaurs are separated into groups based on what time period they lived (Jurassic, Triassic, or Cretaceous), what they ate, where they lives, and what they looked like.

Ornithischia

Thyreophora: Also known as the armored dinosaurs, these dinos were herbivores (plant eaters), and lived in the early Jurassic to the late Creaceous age.

Thyrephora means "shield bearers" because these type of dinosaurs had armors, plates, and horns.

Cerapods: These are typically horned or duck-billed dinosaurs.

They were plant eaters, which had teeth that would grind up the plants to get the most nutrition from it.

Ornithischia

Saurischia

Theropods: The name means "beast feet." They walked on just two legs and were carnivores (meat eaters).

Theropods lived from the late Triassic period till the end of Creaceous age.

The scariest looking and most popular ones in this category were Tyrannosaurus Rex and Veliociraptor.

Sauropods: These lizard-footed type dinosaurs walked on four legs and were enormous in size.

They had long necks and tails, were huge in size, except for their heads, which were fairly small.

The Biggest Dinosaurs

Liopleurodon

#1. Liopleurodon - Liopleurodon looked similar to a whale and a shark.

Paleontologists say that this type of dinosaur weighed over 30 tons and could grow to a length of 50 feet.

#2. Quetzalcoatlus - This type of dinosaur was also huge in size with its wings spanning to 45 feet.

#3. Spinosaurus - Spinosaurus was heavier than T-Rex.

It had a mouth that was similar to crocodile's mouth and it also had a skin flap that stuck out from the back which looked like a sail.

Argentinosaurus - The fossils of this dinosaur were found in Argentina.

It was among the biggest dinosaurs weighting over 100 tons and standing as tall as 120 feet.

Sauroposeidon - This type of dinosaur was very much similar to the Argentinosaurus.

They were about 50 - 60 tons lighter, and their necks are much longer. They cud stretch out to about 40 feet!

Argentinosaurus

The Smallest Dinosaurs

#1. The Humming Bird - It may seem strange but paleontologists believe that dinosaurs did not become extinct completely.

Humming birds are believed to be the relatives of dinosaurs that lived millions of years ago.

It weighs as little as one-tenth of an ounce, and is considered the smallest dinosaur species.

#2. Lariosaurus - They weigh about 20 pounds and are only 2 feet long, this dinosaur was the smallest water dinosaur.

It had a long pointed tail and a straight body.

Lariosaurus (© Wikimedia Commons)

#3. Pterosaurus - Pterosaurus had hollow bones and were lightly built.

They were flying dinosaurs and could be a few inches long up to 40 inches.

This carnivore dinosaur ate insects, crabs, and fish.

#4. Microceratops - The microceratops were the smallest herbivore (plant eating) dinosaur, weighing 4 pounds and they were 1 1/2 feet tall.

#5. Microaptor - The microaptors were the smallest carnivore (meat eating) dinosaurs, standing 2 feet tall.

Microaptor (© Wikimedia Commons)

They were also known as four-winged dinosaur, because they had feathers on their legs and arms.

They ate only insects.

Conclusion

There were many wonderful dinosaurs that roamed the Earth millions of years ago.

I hope you have learned some interesting facts about these animals.

Download Free Books!
http://MendonCottageBooks.com

Purchase at Amazon.com
Website http://AmazingAnimalBooks.com

Our books are available at

1. Amazon.com

2. Barnes and Noble

3. Itunes

4. Kobo

5. Smashwords

6. Google Play Books

Download Free Books!
http://MendonCottageBooks.com

Publisher

JD-Biz Corp

P O Box 374

Mendon, Utah 84325

http://www.jd-biz.com/

Mendon Cottage Books
P O Box 374, Mendon Utah 84325

www.ingramcontent.com/pod-product-compliance
Lightning Source LLC
Chambersburg PA
CBHW050824290526
45792CB00001B/252